PIANO/VOCAL SELECTIONS

SPIDER-MAN
TURN OFF THE DARK

SONGS FROM THE BROADWAY MUSICAL

ISBN 978-1-4584-2478-5

7777 W. Bluemound Rd. P.O. Box 13819 Milwaukee, WI 53213

BOY FALLS FROM THE SKY

Music by U2
Lyrics by BONO and THE EDGE

Gm
3fr
Gm(add4)
3fr
heart knows where you are.
B♭5
G♭
B♭/F
I'd be my - self if I knew who I've be - come.
E♭
3fr
B♭5
You don't have to fly
G♭
B♭/F
E♭
3fr
too high to get too close to the sun.
See the

G♭
B♭
G♭
boy fall from the sky.
Fm
E♭
B♭
G♭
Fm
E♭
3fr
B♭5
E♭m
6fr
Gm
3fr
You will al-ways be in front of me, e-ven as I dis-ap-pear from view,
C5
3fr
B♭5
E♭m
6fr
for I have done not a sin-gle thing with-

Gm
3fr
C/E
B♭5
out the thought of you.
But no,
not here,
not now,
G♭
B♭/F
E♭maj7
3fr
no way.
I'm not read - y to give up the fight.
B♭5
G♭+
B♭/F
If I can use a sin - gle thread to cross the sky,
E♭maj7
3fr
B♭5
G♭+
then why is the eye of the need - le still

B♭/F
E♭
3fr
G♭
your heart to - night.
See how the boy falls
B♭
G♭
Fm
E♭
3fr
from the sky.
B♭
G♭
C♯5
4fr
E5
A5
5fr
Oh,

C♯5
4fr
E5
oh.
G♭5
B♭5
The cit - y con - ducts the sym -
G♭+
B♭/F
- pho - ny; I search through trash for a
E♭
3fr
B♭
mel - o - dy that might lead us back to dig -

G♭+
B♭/F
E♭
3fr
-nity in this junk-yard of hu-man-i-ty. To let
B♭5
G♭6
B♭/F
you go without re-gret. I will for-ev-er hold you al-ways in my
E♭
3fr
B♭5
heart in-stead. O-ver the screams and the
G♭6
B♭/F
si-ren's wail, the on-ly thing not

E♭ B♭5

up for sale. Our love is like lights on a

G♭6 B♭7/F

mid - night train: hearts like thun - der, with no

E♭ B♭5

sound of rain. Light - ning splits the sky,

G♭6 B♭/F

kiss - es your face. Yours is the sac - ri - fice; yours

E♭
3fr
B♭5
is the grace. I hear your voice in -
G♭6
B♭/F
side my head. I will lis - ten to no - bod - y, not to
E♭
3fr
B♭5
no one else. From the bridge where we both stood and
G♭
B♭7/F
stole the view, I saw the you in me, and the

E♭
3fr
B♭
me in you. These are the threads that bind, the ones we
G♭
B♭7/F
have to weave. They will hold us true, I
E♭
3fr
B♭
believe. I be-lieve, I be-lieve,
G♭
B♭/F
be-lieve,

E♭
3fr
B♭
be - lieve,
be - lieve,
be - lieve,
G♭
B♭7/F
E♭
3fr
be - lieve,
be - lieve,
ow!
B♭
G♭
B♭/F
E♭
3fr
B♭5
molto rit.

RISE ABOVE 1

Music and Lyrics by
BONO and THE EDGE

Gm
B♭
F
And you said rise a - bove. I can't,
D7
Gm
I can't. How long will it take
Gm/F
Cm7
be - fore these feel - ings go a - way?
E♭maj7
F
Gm
How much long - er do I wait?

Gm/F
Cm7
3fr
And are there an - y real an - swers an - y - way?
E♭maj7
3fr
F
Gm
3fr
I still can feel your si - lence in a crowd - ed room,
Gm/A
3fr
B♭6
loud - er than the loud - est tune.
Cm
3fr
Gm
3fr
I hang on ev - 'ry word. And you said rise

Bb
F
above,
o - pen your eyes
Cm
Gm
3fr
up.
And you said rise
Bb
F
D7
above.
I can't
I can't.
I
N.C.
miss you in ev - 'ry - thing.
I was too fast trav -

- el - ing to take you in. I know

Gm Gm/F

si - lence is no crime; I just wish I could hear you fill

Cm Cm7 E♭ F

it up one more time. Yes, I

Gm Gm/A

know what you'd say to me, ex -

B♭6
Cm
3fr
act - ly what you'd say to me.
I still hang on ev - 'ry word.
Gm
3fr
B♭
And you said rise a - bove,
F
Cm
3fr
o - pen your eyes
up.
to love.
Gm
3fr
B♭
And you said rise a - bove

F
D7
1
Gm
3fr
your - self.
3
(In a time of trea -
3
B♭
F
son, is there time for trust?
Where there's no them,
Cm
3fr
Gm
3fr
on - ly us,
is there time for rea -
B♭
F
son?
Has your heart had e-nough?
Is it time to let go

D7
2
and rise a - bove?)
B♭
F
Cm
3fr
Up,
up,
Gm
3fr
B♭
up,
up,
F
D7
up,
up.

PICTURE THIS

Music and Lyrics by
BONO and THE EDGE

Moderately fast
N.C.
mf
A5
5fr
A
Em7
PETER PARKER/
SPIDERMAN:
Pic - ture this.
F♯m7
A
O - pen the i - ris, o - pen it up wide.

Em7
The world chang - es shape with the
F♯m7
A
Em7
col - or of your eyes.
Pic - ture this:
F♯m7
A
you are al - read - y where you wan - na be.
Em7
Now close your eyes.
What does it

F♯m7
A
A5
5fr
look like?
A
Dm/A
Em
Pic - ture this:
the world is spin -
F
F♯m
G/D
- ning on a ti - ny pin.
No - bod - y knows
the

F♯m/C♯
A
dan - ger we're in.
On this sun - ny day,
Em7
C
E7(add4)
let your im - ag - i - na - tion run a - way
A
G6/9
C
on this sun - ny day.
E7(add4)
A
G6/9
Sun - ny days,

C E7(add4) A(add4)

see the fu - ture through the haze.

G6 A(add4) G6

C Gm7 Am7 C

MARY JANE WATSON:

Pic - ture this: I wan - na be - lieve

Gm7

you, and I'm gon - na try, but I

Am7
C
find it hard to see me through your eyes.
Gm7
Am7
C
Picture us.
Re - al - ize
Gm7
this is a diz - zy high and we could fall
Am7
C
and fall and fall and fall.

A5

PETER PARKER/ SPIDERMAN:

On this

A G6/9 C6

sun - ny day, let your im - ag - i - na -

Esus A

- tion run a - way

G6/9 C6 Esus

on this sun - ny day.

A
G6/9
C6
Sun - ny days,
see the fu - ture
Esus
Bsus
through the haze.

B F♯m7 G♯m7 B

Love, ___

is this love? ___

F♯m7

G♯m7 B

(Just crimes, peace wars, true lies.)

On this

(I can see a

F♯m7

sun - ny day, ___

no - ble shame.) (I can see a liv - ing death.) (I can see a

G#m7
4fr
B
on this
heal - ing pain, a pure de - cay, a help - ing hurt, a free - ing jail.)
A6/9
D6
sun - ny day,
(Hate, war, hurt, shame, death, pain, hate, war, hurt, shame, death, pain,
Gmaj9
B
A6/9
on this sun - ny day.
hate, war, hurt, shame, death, shame, hate, war, death, pain, hate, war,
D6
Gmaj9
B5
hate, war, death, hurt, death, war, hurt, pain, death, shame!)
rit.

I JUST CAN'T WALK AWAY
(Say It Now)

Music and Lyrics by
BONO and THE EDGE

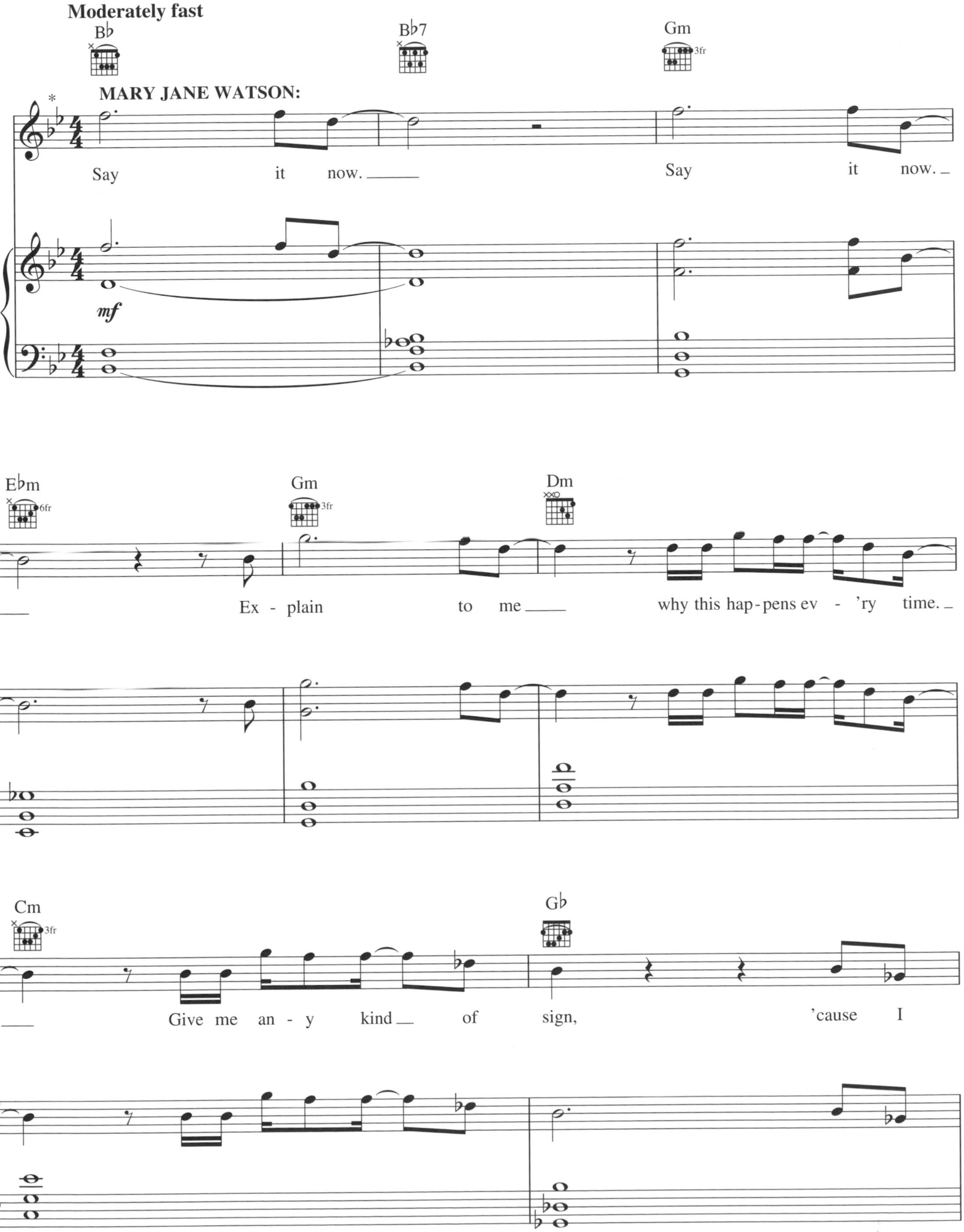

Moderately fast

Bb Bb7 Gm

MARY JANE WATSON:

Say it now. Say it now.

mf

Ebm Gm Dm

Explain to me why this hap-pens ev-'ry time.

* *Recorded a half step higher.*
Vocal line written one octave higher than sung.

B♭
just can't walk a - way.
PETER PARKER/SPIDERMAN:
M.J.W.:
Dm
P.P.:
You wait.
I won't.
I leave.
A♭
4fr
M.J.W.:
E♭
3fr
P.P.:
B♭
I don't.
I mem-o-rize
what I
Dm
A♭
4fr
M.J.W.:
have to say,...
...but he does - n't say it

F(add4)
3fr
an - y - way.
B♭
B♭/A♭
Gm
3fr
BOTH:
Say it now.
Say it now.
E♭m6/9
4fr
G♭maj13
Gm
3fr
Ex - plain to me
Dm
Cm
3fr
why this hap-pens ev - 'ry time.
Give me a clue or tell me why.

Gbmaj7
Gb6
I just can't walk a - way.
Bbm
Bbm/Ab
6fr
(Walk, walk a - way.)
Gbmaj7
Bbm/Eb
(Walk, walk a - way.)
Bb
Dm
P.P.:
Need - ing,... ...ly - ing... Right
M.J.W.: ...ach - ing,... ...a - wake in a room in my heart...

Ab
Eb
here you stay,... ...yet we're miles a - part.
a heart - beat a - way,...
Bb
Dm
BOTH:
You know that love can't live with - out hon - es - ty,
P.P.:
but there's
Ab(add2)
F(add4)
dan - gers in the day - light and the shad - ows with me.
Bb
Bb/Ab
P.P.:
Say it now.
M.J.W.: (Say,...)
BOTH:
I wish I could say

Gm
3fr
E♭m
6fr
it now.
Gm
3fr
Dm
Say to me the words I need to hear,
Cm
3fr
G♭maj7
M.J.W.: (...and why I
why you just don't dis - ap - pear,
P.P.: and why I
G♭6
B♭
just can't walk ...a - way.)
just can't walk.
Say it now.

B♭/A♭
Gm
BOTH:
Say it now.
E♭m
Gm
Say to me
Dm
Cm
the sim-ple words I fear.
I know why I'm here:
G♭maj7
G♭6
P.P.:
BOTH:
'cause I just can't walk a - way.

Bbm
Bbm/Ab
6fr
Gbmaj7
(Walk,
walk a - way.)
Ebsus2
1, 2
3
Ped.

BOUNCING OFF THE WALLS

Music and Lyrics by
BONO and THE EDGE

Edim (3fr)

some - thing has just turned on a light in me.

F♯dim (9fr)

I feel a force flow through ev - ery ar - ter - y now.

A G A F♯dim (9fr)

I can't get down; I

Edim (3fr)

walk up on the roof a - gain, 'round and 'round,

F♯dim
9fr
spin - ning on the spot a - gain. I can't ex - plain the
A
G
A
who, the where, the why or the when now.
G5
3fr
A5
5fr
D5
5fr
E5
And I feel it in my veins. It's a feel -
C5
3fr
D5
5fr
G5
3fr
A5/E
E5
G5
3fr
A5
5fr
D5
5fr
- ing I can't tame. Can an - y - one please ex - plain

E5 C5 D5 G5 A5/E E5

why, why, why, why I'm

E A5 G6 Fmaj7 E

bounc - ing off the walls, bounc - ing off the walls,

A5 G6 Fmaj7 E

bounc - ing off the walls,

A5 G6 Fmaj7 E A5 G6 Fmaj7

bounc - ing off the walls.

F♯dim
9fr
A sun - spot, I'm a - tom - ic en - er - gy.
Edim
3fr
The at - om split, but left the best part of me.
F♯dim
9fr
It's not stat - ic; just e - lec - tri - ci - ty. Wow!
A
G
A
whoa, whoa!

1, 2
E
A5
5fr
G6
Fmaj7
Bounc - ing off the walls.
3
Bounc - ing off the walls.
C5
3fr
G
A
Oh,
oh,

G
A
D(add4)
3fr
and I feel
E5
it in my soul,
what I need
to con - trol.
And I feel
G5
3fr
A5
5fr
D5
5fr
E5
it in my bones.
Let's rock and

C5
D5
G5
A5
E
3fr
5fr
3fr
5fr
N.C.
roll, roll, roll, roll, roll.
E
A5
G6
Fmaj7
5fr
Bounc - ing off the walls.
E
1
A5
G6
Fmaj7
5fr
Bounc - ing off the walls.

2
A5
5fr
G6
Fmaj7
E
A5
5fr
G6
Fmaj7
E
A5
5fr
G6
Fmaj7
E
A5
5fr
G6
Fmaj7
E5
Yeah, yeah, yeah, yeah,
Bdim
B
Al - right!

PULL THE TRIGGER

Music and Lyrics by
BONO and THE EDGE

Moderately

B5 A5 B5 C5 B5 A5 B5 C5

f

B5 A5 B5 C5 Asus2 B♭5

NORMAN OSBORN/ THE GREEN GOBLIN: Spi - der-Man?

VIPER EXECUTIVES: Spi - der-Man? En -

Bm

hanced ge-net-ics.

N.O.: Spi - der - Man.

V.E.: Su-per - hu-man ki-net-ics. A

N.O.: Spi-der-Man.

V.E.: Mus-cle aug - ment - a-tion. And look at that: web

Bm/A Bm/F♯

bi - o - gen er - a - tion.

N.O.: This looks like my work.

Bm
VIPER EXEC 1:
VIPER EXEC 2:
VIPER EXEC 3:
V.E. 1:
N.O.:
It's getting out.
Your life's work.
Your precious research,...
...getting sold!
It is - n't
Bm/A
Bm/F♯
V.E.:
N.O.:
V.E.:
pos - si - ble.
Is - n't it?
It's
not.
Or is it?
B5
A5
B5
C5
B5
A5
B5
C5
May - be it was Kas - si - dy.
You re - lied on loy - al - ty.
B5
A5
B5
C5
A5
F♯5
V.E. 4:
All your staff: where did they go,
and what did they take,
and what did they know? Our

B5
A5
B5
C5
B5
V.E. 1:
A5
B5
C5
V.E. 3:
fund-ing dried up. They were'nt get-ting paid. How's it feel to be be-trayed? They're
F♯5
V.E. 2:
V.E. 1:
V.E.:
leav-ing, like rats from a sink-ing ship. You're los-ing con-trol. You're let-ting it slip. Time to
get it! You've been stabbed in the back! Are you gon-na roll o-ver, play dead, or at-
SOLDIERS:
tack? Wake

B5
up, son. Some-one's cheat-ing you. You do have com-pe-ti-tion, and they're beat-ing you; so
A5
F♯5
fight back! Are you just gon-na wait? It's an arms race, boy, you can't hes-i-tate. We want
B5
N.O.:
new men, a new breed of Ma-rines. Not hu-man, we want fight-ing ma-chines. A new
SOLDIERS:
N.O.:
A5
SOLDIERS:
F♯5
One that's hard-er to kill. We'll get some-one who will.
spe-cies? And what if I won't?

Gmaj7
D6
C♯5
4fr
SOLDIERS:
Don't just think of you.
Bm
Bm/E
Gmaj7
Think of God and coun - try.
Join the
D6
C♯5
4fr
Bm
proud and few
who know best for their coun -
Bm/E
Gmaj7
- try.
Get some pa - tri - ot - ic pride or

A(add2)
B5
A5
B5
C5
5fr
3fr
V.E. 1:
SOLDIERS:
get on to the oth - er side.
How do we win?
By liv-ing in fear!
V.E. 2:
SOLDIERS:
How do we win?
Get the en - e - my clear!
V.E. 3:
SOLDIERS:
How do we win?
By say-ing it's done
F♯5
in re - tal - i - a - tion!
How do we win?
By clear-ing them out!
How do we win?
By mur-der and doubt!
How do we win?
'Cause we're in the right!

Asus2
Bm/F♯
B5
Get in line, or say good - night!
B5
A5
B5
C5
5fr
3fr
Guitar solo ad lib.
B5
A5
B5
C5
5fr
3fr
B5
A5
B5
C5
5fr
3fr
A5
5fr
F♯5
Gmaj7
D6
C♯5
4fr
Play 4 times
ENSEMBLE:
Last time (Solo ends)
Don't just think of you: _

Bm
Bm/E
think of God and coun - try.
Gmaj7
D6
C♯5
4fr
Join the proud and few who
Bm
Bm/E
know best for their coun - try.
Gmaj7
A(add2)
SOLDIERS:
Get some pa - tri - ot - ic pride or get on to the oth - er side.
So de -

B5 A5 B5 C5 B5 A5 B5 C5

N.O.: liv - er! **SOLDIERS:** We want **N.O.:** big - ger! **SOLDIERS:** Pull the

(I ain't work - ing for you.) _ (That ain't some - thing I do.) _

B5 A5 B5 C5 A5 F♯5

trig - ger; start be - ing a man, _ Take care of bus-'ness or get off the can. Start

B5 A5 B5 C5 B5 A5 B5 C5

mak - ing and you'll be in con - trol! Start tak - ing! **N.O.:** (You wan - na suck out my soul?) **SOLDIERS:** Get

B5 A5 B5 C5 A5 F♯5

SOLDIERS: fund - ed! ...Or your ba - by won't live! **N.O.:** I'm gon - na say no! **SOLDIERS:** You mean, "af - firm - a - tive!" Yes

B7(no3)
(Hut! Hut! Hut! Hut! Hut! Hut! Hut, two, three!)
sir! Yes sir! Yes sir! Yes sir!
A5
5fr
F♯5
(Hut! Hut! Hut! Hut! Hut! Hut! Hut, two, three!)
Yes
B7(no3)
(Hut! Hut! Hut! Hut! Hut! Hut! Hut, two, three!)
sir! Yes sir! Yes
A5
5fr
F♯5
B5
N.O.:
(Hut! Hut! Hut! Hut! Hut! Hut! Hut, two, three!)
sir!
Spoken: Spider-Man!

NO MORE

Music and Lyrics by
BONO and THE EDGE

Moderately
B♭m
PETER PARKER/
SPIDERMAN:
E♭
3fr
B♭m
Don't talk, just walk. Go - in' nuts,
mf
G♭
B♭m
E♭
3fr
hate my guts. Get good grades, an - oth - er shove.
B♭m
G♭
B♭m
Stop be-ing a los - er, stop be - ing in love. And why do I need these

E♭ B♭m E♭

stu - pid glass - es. I'd give my life to be

Gm G

any - one but me, yeah,

Gm G Gm

an - y - one but me. I wan - na be an - y - one but me,

G Gm C/G

yeah.

Eb/G
Cm7
Gm
Em
MARY JANE WATSON:
This is - n't home; just a house.
A
Em
C
Bro - ken door, bro - ken glass. Dad - 'll yell. Tune him out. He's drunk by now; he has to
Em
A
Em
shout. Keep on walk - ing; just ig - nore; just get to your room and
C
Em
Asus2
shut the door. Let me dis - ap - pear, or just be

A5
D♭m
D♭
an - y - where but here, yeah.
D♭m
D♭
D♭m
An - y - where but here, I wan - na be.
G5
Cm6
Cm13
G
G5
P.P.:
Ev - 'ry day is like a

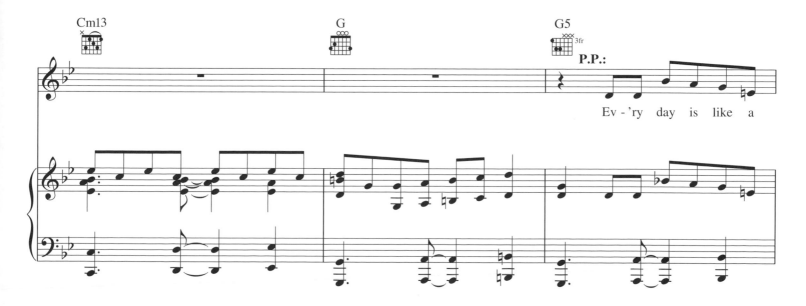

Cm6
Cm13
G
war, and I'm los - ing it. I'm tak - ing hits from ev - 'ry side, ev - 'ry side that there is.
G5
Am
Cm6
M.J.W.:
Ev - 'ry day I feel the walls are clos - ing in. When can I begin to
G
F
C/E
G
BOTH:
P.P.:
get my - self right out of this place. An - y - one but me. (I count the grass as it grows.
F
C/E
G
Dsus4(add2)
M.J.W.:
P.P.:
An - y - where but here. I go to sleep in my clothes, but the

G
G/B
P.P.:
shoes don't fit.) I am not what I've been told; I
M.J.W.: (Where do I live?)
C
E/G♯
Am
am not what I've been sold. I'm at the point of pos - si -
(What do I take?)
B♭
F
bil - i - ty. I can al - most glimpse in -
(Who will I find?) (What - ev - er sign?)
C/E
Am7
D
BOTH:
fi - ni - ty. I am not where I be - long. And
(When is my time?) (Is it now?)

F
G
Am7
I can see an o - pen door.
And I can't live like this
D/F♯
F
C/E
G
no more.
I can't live like this
no more.
F
C/E
G
D5
Dsus
Dm7
I can't live like this
no more.
No, no, no,
D5
Dsus
Dm7
D5
Dsus
Dm7
Dsus4(add2)
no, no, no, no, no, no more.

DIY WORLD

Music and Lyrics by
BONO and THE EDGE

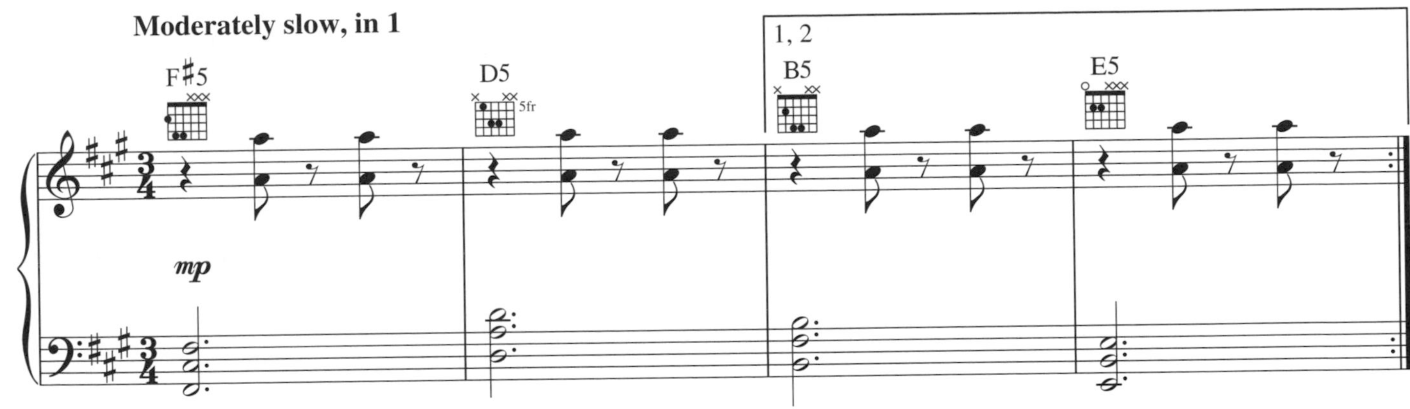

Bm
B
D
N.O.:
To - mor - row be - longs to the
H.S. STUDENTS & LAB ASSISTANTS:
D. I. Y. world. 'Cause we can be what we wan - na be,
Bm7
E6
F♯m
D
brave: not the slave, but the brave.
and we need to be what we got - ta be, do it your- self, do it your- self,
Bm
B
Am
Fm
N.O.:
D. I. Y. world. Gam - ma rays, ti - dal waves,

Am
C5
3fr
A♭
4fr
Am
in - flu - en - za, there's so man - y ways the hu - man race can
Fm
E5
N.C.
Am
take a hit. We're gon - na sink, but
Fm
Am
C5
3fr
A♭
4fr
you can swim if you don't mind a lit - tle change of skin. De - sign - er
Am
Fm
E5
F♯m
H.S. STUDENTS & LAB ASSISTANTS:
jeans are a bet - ter fit. 'Cause we can be
N.C.

D
Bm7
E6
F♯m
what we wan - na be, and we need to be what we got - ta be, that's what we ought - a
D
Bm7
B
Bm/F♯
EMILY OSBORN:
To - mor - row be -
N.O. & PETER PARKER/SPIDERMAN:
To - mor - row be -
be in the D. I. Y. world. 'Cause we can be
Bm7
E6
F♯m
longs to the brave, all to the brave.
longs to the brave: not the slave, but the brave.
what we wan - na be, and we need to be what we got - ta be, do it your - self,

D
Bm7
B
Am
P.P.:
do it your - self, D. I. Y. world.
Ris - ing seas, _
Fm
LAB ASSISTANT:
Am
Cm
3fr
N.O.:
A♭
4fr
no more trees. _ Could be a freak - in' fleet of kill - er bees! We're mas - ters
Am
Fm
E5
N.C.
of cre - a - tion.

Am
Fm
Am
N.O. & P.P.:
N.O.:
D. N. A. is the way, now that ev - o - lu - tion's
C
A♭
4fr
Am
N.O. & P.P.:
had its way: In - tel - li - gent de - sign so -
Fm
E
N.C.
ENSEMBLE:
lu - tion. And we, we could
F/A
live for a thou - sand

F♯m
D
Bm7
years.
('Cause we can be what we wan - na be, and we need to be
E6
F♯m
D
what we got - ta be, that's what we ought - a be in the
Bm7
B
F♯m
D. I. Y. world.
'Cause we can be
(Do it to your -
D
Bm7
E
what we wan - na be, and we need to be what we got - ta be,
self, to your - self, do it to your - self.

F♯m
D
Bm7
that's what we ought - a be in the D. I. Y.
Do it to your - self, to your - self, do it
B
F♯m
D
Bm7
EMILY OSBORN:
To - mor - row be - longs to the brave,
N.O. & P.P.:
To - mor - row be - longs to the brave: not the
world. 'Cause we can be what we wan - na be, and we need to be
to your - self.) (Do it to your - self, to your - self, do it
E6
F♯m
Dmaj7
all to the brave.
slave, but the brave.
what we got - ta be, do it your - self, do it your - self,
to your - self. Do it to your - self, to your -

Bm7
B
Am
Fm
N.O.: Imagine!
We could produce super strength
D. I. Y. world.
self, do it to your-self.)
Am
Cm
A♭
Am
electric reflexes!
Powers once reserved for the ancient
Fm
E5
N.C.
Dm/F
gods are now within our grasp!
ENSEMBLE:
And we,

B♭
we could live
(We could live . . .)
Dm/A
Gm
3fr
for a thou - sand
F♯m
years!
accel.
rit.
Ped.

IF THE WORLD SHOULD END

Music and Lyrics by
BONO and THE EDGE

Moderately
D5
5fr
B♭maj7
p
MARY JANE WATSON:
Don't think a - bout to - mor - row;
we've on - ly got to -
day.
There's noth - ing that I want from you,
not a word you have to say.
You are all I

A
D5
need, and all I can de - fend,
B♭/D
B♭
A(add4)
all I need to hold on to
if the world should
D5
B♭maj7♭5
B♭maj7
B♭maj13
D5
end.
B♭maj7♭5
B♭maj7
B♭maj13
Dm
In my im - ag - i - na - tion

B♭maj7♭5
B♭maj7
B♭maj13
Bm7♭5
I could not have made this up.
B♭maj7♭5
B♭maj7
B♭maj13
Dm
In a world strang - er than fic - tion,
B♭maj7♭5
B♭maj7
B♭maj13
Bm7♭5
B♭maj7
ours is no fic - tion - al love.
I can see the
Gm
3fr
A(add4)
Dm
Dm/C
you un - der your sec - ond skin;

B♭maj7
Gm
A
I can feel your heart - beat quick - en,
Dm
Dm/C
B♭maj7
Gm
quick - en and then slow. There's noth - ing else I need to
A
B♭maj7
know, and there's noth - ing you need to pre -
A
Gm
tend. If the world should end,

F6 Eb Dm

and the sky to-night is lu - mi - nous for all

A Dm Eb

the wrong rea - sons, and ev - 'ry door - way is

Dm A Bbmaj7 A7(no3)

hid - ing some - thing, and if this world

Bb F A

should all come crash - ing

B♭maj7
B♭
F
down,
I would-n't care
at
A
D5
5fr
all.
And if there's no to - mor-row,
rit.
a tempo
B♭maj7
D5
B♭maj7
I'll have to-day a - gain.
There's no time for
D5
B♭maj7
D5
sor - row
when there's no such thing as time.

B♭maj7
Gm
A(add4)
And if the dark - ness will de- scend,
don't need a sav - ior or
Dm
Dm/C
B♭maj7
Gm
a friend.
I can say I've real - ly loved
A(add4)
Dm
B♭maj7
if the world should end.
rit.
a tempo
Dm
B♭maj7
Dm
rit.

SINISTEREO

Music and Lyrics by
BONO and THE EDGE

Moderately fast
N.C.
E5
f

E5
E5/B
REPORTERS:
Now come thoughts that you
Breath of our breath with
Guitar solo ad lib.

Eb/G 3fr Cm7 3fr C/Bb Em E5/B

shall ___ not ban - ish: ___ se - cret
no blood or bone ___ nev - er grows

Eb/G 3fr Cm7 3fr C/Bb

fears, vi - sions ne'er ___ to van - ish. ___
wear - y, ___ nev - er grows old, ___
(3.) *Guitar solo ends*

Em E5/B

Crawl - ing shapes now ___ come
mut - ters and mum - bles ___ in
Much ___ of mad - ness, ___ and

Eb/G 3fr Cm7 3fr C/Bb

writh - ing out, ___
in - fi - nite ways, ___
more ___ of sin. ___

Em
E5/B
t'cast their shad - ow o - ver this
ev - er the ty - rant to
No gov - ern - ment of this
E♭/G
3fr
Cm7
3fr
C/B♭
E5
E5/B
hu - man rout.
the will - ing slaves.
vast, form-less thing.
Gm6
3fr
C7
B♭(♭5)
You set your - self on fire.
You set your-
E5
E5/B
Gm6
3fr
C7
self on fire.
You set your - self on fire.

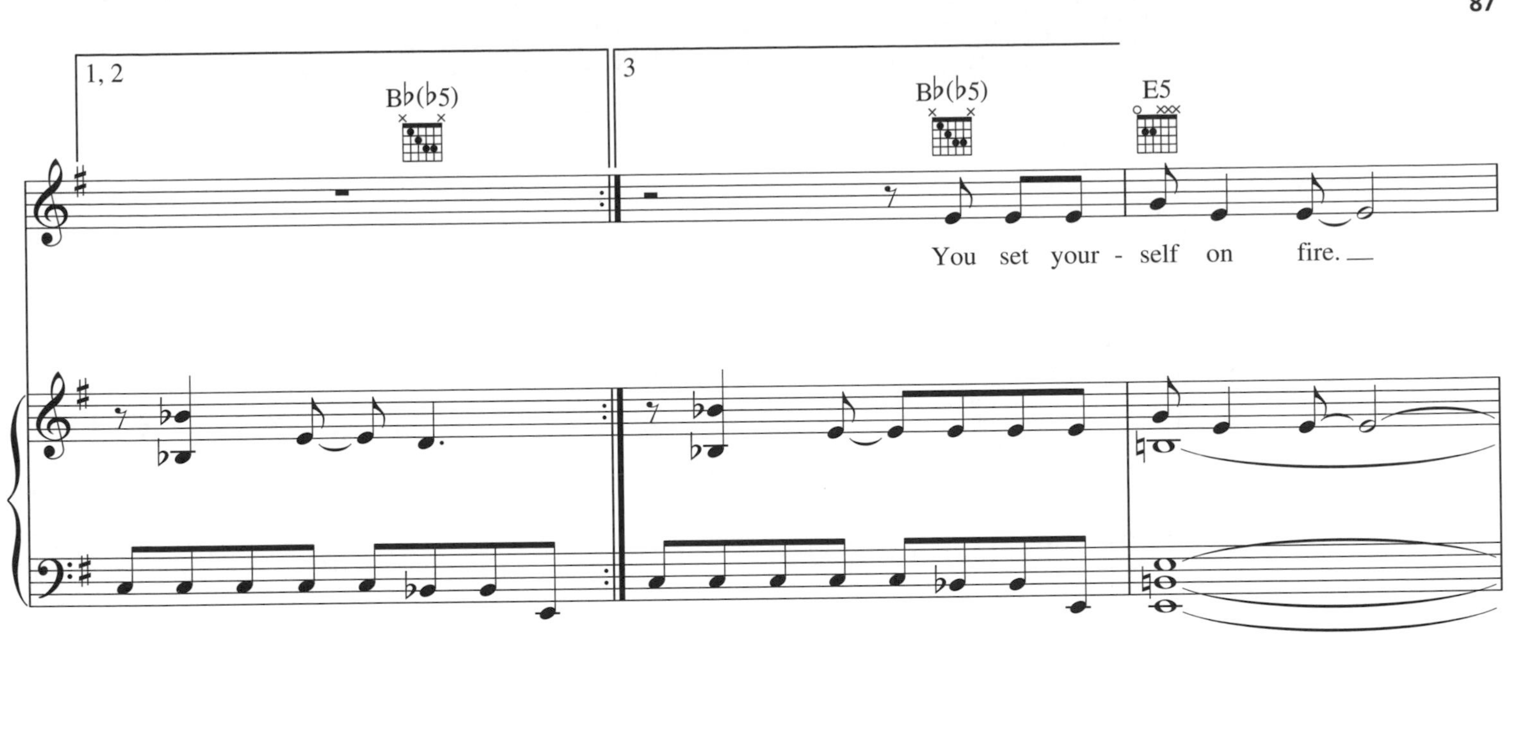
1, 2
Bb(b5)
3
Bb(b5)
E5
You set your - self on fire.

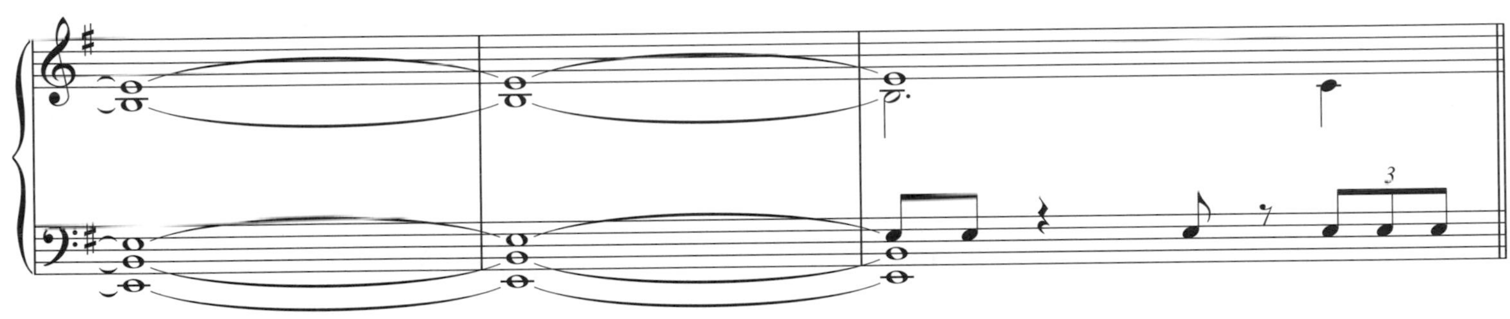
3

E5
E5/B
Gm6
3fr
C7

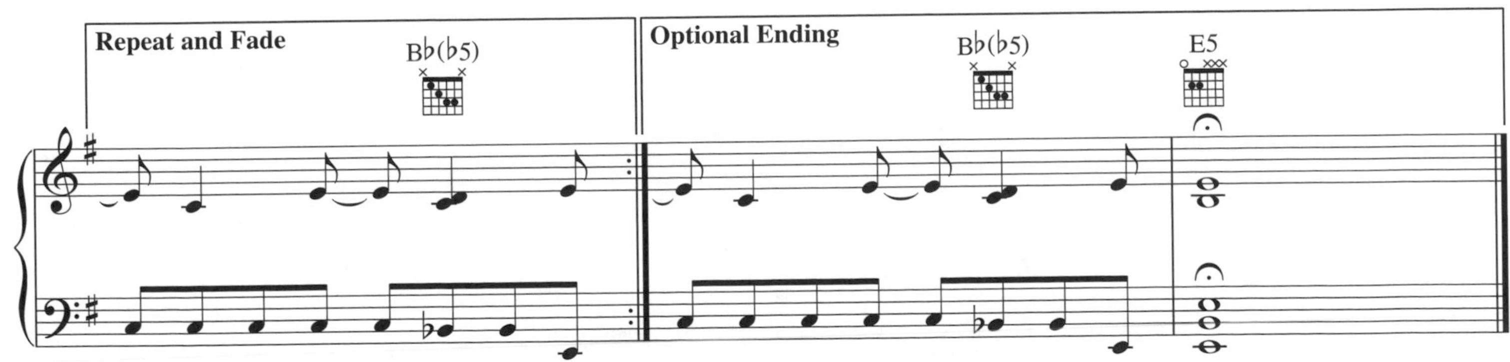
Repeat and Fade
Bb(b5)
Optional Ending
Bb(b5)
E5

A FREAK LIKE ME NEEDS COMPANY

Music and Lyrics by
BONO and THE EDGE

Am G Am/G
six - ty - five mil - lion dol - lar cir - cus trag - e - dy.
(A freak like me needs
Dm Am/G Am G
I'm not roll - in', ba - by, roll - in' in the green, but I'm u - nique,
com - pa - ny.)
Am/G Dm G5 Am
3fr
a freak. I'm the new Co - ney Is - land, and all
(Freak.) (Freak!)
G Am/G Dm
the rides are o - pen and free. On me!
(A freak like me needs com - pa - ny.)

Bm
D
A
C♯m/G♯
ENSEMBLE:
All the weir - dos in the world are here right now in
F♯7(no3rd)
G♯dim
D6
D6/C♯
E
New York Cit - y. All the braz - en boys and girls
girls,
dressed to kill with - out
pea - cocks, pos - ers show no
pit - y. All the weir - dos from
out of town, and all the freaks al - ways a - round;

To Coda

D6 D6/C♯ E G/A 3fr

all the weir - dos in the world are here in New York

A G/A 3fr A

Cit - y to - night, here in New York Cit - y to - night.

Am G6

D5 5fr G Am Am/G

GREEN GOBLIN FLYER:

I got a crew of par - ty an - i - mal mu - tants by ___ my side: _

ENSEMBLE: (A

G
D5
D/G
Am
5fr
De - mon hair - do, e - vil dress - ers who just
freak like me needs com - pa - ny.)
Am/G
G
D5
Gsus2
won't be de - nied.
The
(A freak like me needs com - pa - ny.)
Am
Am/G
cross - roads of the world just needs a lit - tle
G
D5
D/G
tweak from a freak.
I've said
(Tweak from a freak!)

Am
Am/G
good - bye to my straight life, 'cause I
(A
G
D5
5fr
D/G
D.S. al Coda
love a freak.
freak like me needs com - pa - ny.)
CODA
G/A
3fr
A
here in New York Cit - y to - night,
G/A
3fr
A
MALE CHORUS:
here in New York Cit - y to - night. Oh.

Am
Am/G
Oh,
1
2
Dm
Am/G
oh.
Oh.
oh.
Oh.
G.G.F.: (Oh yeah.)
Am
Am/G
Oh,
(That's the boys.)
Dm
Am/G
Am
Am/G
FEMALE CHORUS:
oh.
Oh.
La, la, la, la,
(And the la - dies sing:)

Dm Am/G Am

la, la, la, la, la, la, la, la, la, la.

Am/G Dm Am/G

La, la, la, la, la, la, la, la, la, la, la, la, la, la.

Am G

La, la, la, la, la, la, la, la, la,

D Am

la, la, la, la, la. La, la, la, la.

RISE ABOVE 2

Music and Lyrics by
BONO and THE EDGE

Moderately
B♭6
Gm
mf
PETER PARKER/
SPIDERMAN:
When the ones who run the fire - house are the ones who start the fire, and the law - less make the laws, and ev - 'ry preach - er is a li - ar, and the ones that damn the in - no - cent, well, they
3fr
E♭maj7

F6 Bb6

own the night - ly news and front page.

An old man said to me, "It's not

Gm

who, but what you know; and know-ledge is - n't wis - dom with -

Ebmaj7

out con - trol. Bet - ter still to be the chang - es that you

Gm/F
B♭6
wan - na see. __ They come slow, I know"
Gm
B♭
And you said rise __ a - bove;
F/A
Cm
Gm
o - pen your eyes up. __ And you said rise _
B♭
F/A
D7
__ a - bove, but I can't, I can't. _

Am
F6
Fmaj7
MARY JANE WATSON:
For
Cm
Cm/B♭
ev - 'ry heart that bleeds will col - or your world red, and the
A♭maj7
Gsus
G
sor - row in the night will be the blue you can - not shed. But your
Cm
Cm/B♭
strength will be a vi - sion be - yond vis - i - bil - i - ty, and the

A♭maj7
G
G7
gift you have with - in will give you new eyes to see.
Cm
E♭
B♭/D
And you can rise a - bove, swing through the skies
Fm
Cm
E♭
a - bove. And you shall rise a - bove
B♭/D
G
B♭m
your - self. Know that I'll be

Fm
B♭m
Fm
watch - ing. Know that I'll be wait - ing.
A♭
4fr
P.P.:
Stand - ing on the prec - i - pice, I can soar a - way from
3
Cm
3fr
E♭
3fr
B♭/D
P.P.:
this. (Free your soul.)
ENSEMBLE:
And you can rise a - bove. O - pen your eyes

Fm
Cm
3fr
(Rise a-bove your-self and take con - trol.)
3
up.
And you can rise
3
Eb
3fr
Bb/D
(You need to love,
to re-
a - bove
your - self.
G
G7
Cm
3fr
Eb
3fr
P.P. & M.J.W.:
lease your-self and rise a-bove it all.)
3
(I will be there.)
And you can rise a - bove.
3

Bb/D
Fm
Cm
M.J.W.:
(You were nev - er a - lone.)
O - pen your eyes up.
And you can rise
Eb
Bb/D
G
P.P. & M.J.W.:
(In - side your dreams,
I've been watching and wait - ing for you.)
a - bove your - self.
Cm
Eb
Bb/D
M.J.W.:
And you can rise a - bove,
o - pen your eyes
And you can rise a - bove,
o - pen your eyes

Fm
Cm
3fr
E♭
3fr
to love.
And you can rise above
up.
And you can rise above
B♭/D
G
your - self.
your - self.
3
rit.
G♯m
4fr
P.P.:
And ev - 'ry heart that bleeds will
a tempo

G♯m/F♯
4fr
Emaj7
col - or your world red, and the sor - row in the night will be the
D♯7
G♯m
4fr
3
blue you can - not shed. And your strength will be a vi - sion be -
G♯m/F♯
4fr
Emaj7
3
yond vis - i - bil - i - ty, and the gift you have be - fore you will give you
G♯m/C♯
4fr
G♯m
4fr
new eyes to see.
rit.

TURN OFF THE DARK

Music and Lyrics by
BONO and THE EDGE

*Written an octave higher than sung.

B
F♯m
in the shad - ow - land,
in the shad - ow - land,
A
C
G
turn of the dark,
turn off the
Bm
A(add2)
dark.
Be - tween the
Amaj9/C♯
D6/9
4fr
look - ing and the see - ing,
be - tween the

F♯m7
A(add2)
hurt - ing and the weep - ing, be - tween the
Amaj9/C♯
B7sus
2fr
wak - ing and the sleep - ing, are
E(add4)/F♯
A(add2)
you sleep - ing? Ah. Turn off the
C
D
A
dark, oh, yeah, yeah.
3
3

C6
C
Turn off the dark,,
3
3
G
Bm11
Very freely
turn off the dark.
I've been
molto rit.
wait - ing.
I've been
3
Tempo I
F♯m11
wait - ing.
Spoken: I am the queen of dreams,

Amaj13
Amaj9/G♯
banished to a shadow prison.
But I've watched and waited as your powers have risen,
F♯m11
and now my loneliness can be undone,
for the fates have delivered you, my one.
Amaj13
Amaj9/G♯
With me alone, you have nothing to hide.
Confide in me;...
F♯m
...inside of me, the universe awaits.
Unwind... we'll eclipse this mortal mind.

Amaj13 Amaj9/G♯

The gift you've been given binds you to me with spider silk threads,

F♯m11

across the galaxy.

A(add2)

Repeat and Fade

F♯m11

Optional Ending

F♯m11